Sophie Macheteau

Purrfection

How to Achieve Balance and Happiness Through Your Cat

4880 Lower Valley Road · Atglen, PA 19310

Copyright © 2018 by Schiffer Publishing, Ltd.

Originally published as *Chaton Therapie* © 2016 by Rustica, a subsidiary of Fleurus Éditions, Paris. Translated from the French by Omicron Language Solutions, LLC.

Studio les Trois Becs
Audio recording and mastering:
Pierre Palengat, Studio les Trois Becs

Library of Congress Control Number:
2017953859

Photo credits:
Cover photo: Getty Images/Benjamin Torode. Interior photos: iStockphoto, except for pages 35, 72, 75, 77, 79, 81, 86: Thomas Léaud (model: Léa Didier); Pages 8, 65, 88-90: Sophie Macheteau. Illustrations pages 55, 57–58: Lise Herzog.

Editing director: Elisabeth Pegeon
Editor: Juliette Magro
Text preparation: Hélène Fitamant-Gaudin
Design concept: Mathieu Tougne

Cover design by Danielle Farmer
Designed by Brenda McCallum
Type set in Daydreamer/Avenir

ISBN: 978-0-7643-5501-1
Printed in China

Published by Schiffer Publishing, Ltd.
4880 Lower Valley Road
Atglen, PA 19310
Phone: (610) 593-1777
Fax: (610) 593-2002
E-mail: Info@schifferbooks.com
Web: www.schifferbooks.com

For our complete selection of fine books on this and related subjects, please visit our website at www.schifferbooks.com. You may also write for a free catalog.

Schiffer Publishing's titles are available at special discounts for bulk purchases for sales promotions or premiums. Special editions, including personalized covers, corporate imprints, and excerpts, can be created in large quantities for special needs. For more information, contact the publisher.

We are always looking for people to write books on new and related subjects. If you have an idea for a book, please contact us at proposals@schifferbooks.com.

Contents

One of a Kind!

Satisfaction

Between the Two of us

Cyber Cat

Kitty Fashion

For Cats' Sake!

Foreword

I admire Nature, I appreciate
its beauty, as in this little
feline we've been favored
with. A cat is refined, it's a
sensitive being; it likes its
freedom and happy hours.
It marks its territory—oh valued horizon!
Its home, like its territory, is sacred. Its
mysterious life is important to it, its reign
is imposing, its comfort vital. For humans
it is an intimate companion, attentive to
movement, its gaze is sublime. Often,
when night falls, it hunts for small rodents
in the darkness; it is a sepulchral night.
A blessed animal, the cat is marvelous;
it shares our lives and makes us happier.

Yves Macheteau

For
Praline,
Myrtille,
and
Ginger

Françoise Giroud, the famed French politician, journalist, and screenwriter, liked to say that we don't own cats—they own us! If you have the good luck and the privilege to share your daily life with a kind kitty, you will easily understand what she means, as a cat knows how to seduce us and lead us by the nose. A unique and almost intense relationship exists between humans and *felidae*, a fur-deep complicity free of speech—a simple glance and we understand each other immediately.

A cat is an ideal companion; it never gets tired of our humor, isn't bothered by our moods, knows how to be patient when necessary, and is always faithful.

As far back as I can remember, I have always been fascinated by and attracted to cats…

When I was 10, I dreamed of becoming a cat tamer in the circus.

When I was 12, I saved a kitten from certain death.

When I was 15, I wanted to become a veterinarian—but only for cats.

When I was 26, I adopted my first cat, an angora with the sweet name of Mogwai.

And a few years later, here I am the happy roommate of three adorable felines, each of which has its own strong character and completely unique personality; the youngest takes an enormous pleasure in bringing me his trophies—"charming" shrews, which I'm secretly terrified of. I had always naively believed that cats chased them away….

These are the reasons I'm now sitting here writing this foreword.

Adopting a cat is a special and marvelous adventure, full of surprises and rebounds. Your relationship with a cat will certainly be rich and unique. I hope that this book will help you to optimize a very feline friendship.

A Glance at Cat History

Since our paths first crossed, about 10,000 years ago, the cat has never left us indifferent. Often venerated, sometimes demonized, it has always had a special place at a human's side. Cats certainly know a lot about human history.

Only Three Species!

Like other domestic animals, modern cats descend from several wild subspecies: *Felis silvestris silvestris*, the European wildcat; *Felis silvestris ornate*, the Asian wildcat; and *Felis silvestris libyca*, the Libyan wildcat, also called the "gloved" cat, which is native to the Mediterranean rim, Africa, and the Middle East.

The Cat in Antiquity

It was long believed that domesticating cats began in Ancient Egypt, but that was without taking into account an archeological discovery dating back to the year 7500 BCE, which revealed a burial chamber of a man accompanied by a cat, a cat that according to the offerings present had been domesticated.

No matter what, the cohabitation and special closeness between humans and cats seems to coincide with the beginning of agriculture; the storage of grain attracted rodents, which in turn were followed by their natural predators.

Egypt in Roman times appears to have been the distribution vector of cats. The animals were domesticated in the Nile Valley between 3000 and 1500 BCE. Deified, the cat quickly became a sacred animal, forbidden for people to touch. Killing a cat carried the death penalty, and to prove love and devotion toward the animal, a cat would be mummified after its death and placed in a sarcophagus.

Felis silvestris libyca

The Egyptians worshipped cats in the form of the goddess Bastet, symbol of fecundity, joy, music, and maternal love. She was represented in the shape of a cat or as a woman with a cat's head.

The Cat in Roman Times

With the rise to power of the Ptolemaic Dynasty and the abandoning of pagan cultures imposed by Theodosius, the first Roman and Byzantine Emperor, the cat lost its divine role and privileged position. However, it continued to be domesticated and defend grain stores against the threat of rodents. At first reserved for the rich, the cat quickly spread throughout the Empire and to every social class.

One Cat May Conceal Another...

If you think that our favorite feline has always been called a cat, you are wrong! It was given different names according to different epochs.

Here are some examples:

- Ancient Greece, the cat was called *ailouros*, meaning "animal that wags its tail."

- In Ancient Egypt, the male cat was called *mau* after the onomatopoeia of its meow; the female was called *techau*.

- During the era of the Roman Empire, the cat was called *felis*, referring to its species.

- At the beginning of the fourth century, just before the start of the Middle Ages, the cat was called *cattus*, meaning "sensible."

- During the Middle Ages, several names were used, each beginning with *mus*, signifying "mouse."

- The Old English word *catt* dates back to the eight century.

The Medieval Cat

By the start of the Middle Ages, the cat had become a widely-found animal throughout Europe. During a large part of this period, it continued to be appreciated for its hunting talents.

In the Flames of Hell…

"Lucifer can appear to his followers and worshippers in the shape of a black cat or a toad, and demand kisses from them; the former is abominable, […] the latter horrific."

—Bishop William of Auvergne (died 1249), *On Faith and Law*

It was during the second half of the twelfth century that the cat began to be linked with the devil. This association increased at the beginning of the thirteenth century, when Cathars and other heretic sects were accused of worshipping Satan disguised as a cat. Immediately, church leaders began to spread a negative image of cats, considering them to reflect human vices.

The Cat's Nine Lives

According to an ancient belief that started among the Egyptians, cats were able to escape from death a certain number of times (due to their incredible suppleness and their ability to land on their feet) and to live several lives.

Why nine lives? Possibly because the number 9 was a mystical number believed to bring happiness and to hold supernatural power, traits also attributed to cats.

In the fourteenth century, cats were systematically associated with sorcery. In an era where Christianity was in full swing, the strong sexual appetite of this animal, its night vision, and its intense need for sleep (!) suddenly made it appear to be an evil creature. To make matters worse for our feline friends, at each new wave of suppression, wizards and witches confessed to having seen the devil incarnated as a cat. Cats were accused of having every vice: greed, perfidy, laziness, oversexualization, and even insanity. The black cat was the worst of the lot!

Without any chance to defend themselves, cats were condemned to be burned at the stake, the same fate assigned to people accused of witchcraft. And there was another myth that witches turned into cats to suck the lifeblood out of children.

The Church's distrust of cats resulted in a spiritual and moral rule requiring the relationship between human and animal to be limited to strict subordination. In this, an animal must not be a companion for someone—because not only could it push him into sin, but also the caresses lavished on it were so sensual that they were suspicious.

Thus the cat as the devil and the cat changing shape have been a part of Western imagination up to the present.

More Than One Way to Skin a Cat

As sordid as it might seem, during the Middle Ages trade in cat-skin was frequent, as we can see by some proverbs: "I don't want a cat, except for its skin" (fifteenth century); "You can trust someone saying he's got the cat when you see him holding the cat skin" (around 1470).

The Cat as Healer

Apart from its fur, people were also interested in cats for their medicinal qualities. Up until the eleventh century, cat excrement was used in medical concoctions, mainly used to cure ulcers and lower fever, as Pliny suggested, but also to stop encroaching baldness. Sextus noted the recipe for an ointment composed of equal parts of crushed dried cat excrement and wild mustard, steeped in vinegar.

The Cat Regains Its Status

"Man is civilized to the extent that he understands cats."

—George Bernard Shaw
(1856–1950)

As the Renaissance got underway, cats were still being accused of every vice. They were also associated with feminity and sexuality. In the sixteenth century numerous cats were sacrificed during festivities, such as the bonfires on Saint John's Eve.

Mummified cats found during the demolition of buildings attests to a custom practiced during the Middle Ages and beginning of the Renaissance: burying black cats in the foundations, presumably to stop the devil from entering the building. A cruel way of paying tribute to Satan…

It took a long time for the cat to become respected and valued once more. At the start of the sixteenth century, the feline's gradual return to good favor began, though they weren't unanimously tolerated. Among the cat's friends was the high-ranking Cardinal Richelieu, who admitted a true admiration for cats and who possessed fourteen at the end of his life. As for King Louis XIV, in 1648, he declared a ban on throwing cats into bonfires on Saint John's Eve. Progress!

From the seventeenth century on, cat lovers showed themselves in literature, poetry, and even politics. The court of France's King Louis XV included several cat lovers, and the king himself had a huge white angora cat. "Puss in Boots,"

Cat Flap? Did You Say Cat Flap?

As we can see from "The Miller's Tale" in *The Canterbury Tales*, where its author Geoffrey Chaucer speaks of "a hole in the bottom of a plank, through which the cat comes and goes," cat flaps already existed in the fourteenth century.

a fairy tale written at the end of the seventeenth century, shows the more respectful connection between people and cats.

In the eighteenth century, cats were helped by a trend toward condemning cruelty to animals. Another thing in their favor was their cleanliness, in an era when hygiene regulations and expectations became stricter.

In the nineteenth century, the growing number of works about cats attested to their place as a pet. The appearance of rare and exotic breeds helped to popularize our beloved felines. They became associated with traits like a secret intelligence, freedom, feminity, and a certain disregard for the rules.

Catty Words

A tuxedo cat is one kind of bicolor cat. Its coloring brings to mind a tuxedo: black with a white bib. Tuxedos may also have some white on the paws, belly, chest, throat, and face.

The Cat

From his brown and yellow fur
Comes such sweet fragrance that one night
I was perfumed with it because
I caressed him once, once only.

A familiar figure in the place,
He presides, judges, inspires
Everything within his province;
Perhaps he is a fey, a god?

When my gaze, drawn as by a magnet,
Turns in a docile way
Toward that cat whom I love,
And when I look within myself

I see with amazement
The fire of his pale pupils,
Clear signal-lights, living opals,
That contemplate me fixedly.

—from *Les Fleurs du mal* (1857), Baudelaire

Cats Rule

In the Land of the Rising Sun

Cats in offices, venerated statues, neko cafés that never empty, and a cat island that fascinates everyone… We can safely say that the Japanese devote themselves to felines, and the cat culture there doesn't show signs of flagging.

Maneki Neko, a Cult Figurine

It's impossible to talk about cats in Japan without mentioning the famous Maneki Neko (literally, "cat that invites"). This traditional figurine made of porcelain or ceramic represents a cat sitting down with one paw raised at ear level. Also called the "lucky cat" or the "beckoning cat," it is supposed to bring wealth when the right paw is raised, and good luck when the left paw is raised…too bad both paws aren't raised at the same time!

Several legends surround the origins of this good-luck feline. One tells of a samurai who came across a cat which seemed to be beckoning to him. He left his path and approached the cat, thus avoiding falling into an ambush set up for him on his initial path. It didn't need any more than that to create the legend of good luck.

You'll frequently see Maneki Neko figurines at the entrance to shops and malls in Japan. It even has its own holiday, celebrated on September 29!

Off to Work!

How does taking your feline to work—with the total support of your boss—sound? That's exactly what the Ferray Corporation, a web design company, has done. It started by adopting nine cats and settling them full-time in its offices to wander about freely. That was successful in terms of encouraging cooperation and productivity among the workforce, so the company also began allowing its employees to bring their pets to work.

Why? The company directors could see that having a pet with you at work led to improved communication among its workers, and also lowered stress levels.

Neko Cafés

These cat cafés are highly successful in Japan, attracting office employees who drop in after work, as well as many younger people. In these kitty bars, you can relax and read *manga* without paying much attention to the cats (except for feeling their beneficial presence), or you can play with them and feed them for a few extra yen. Cat cafés have now popped up in the rest of the world, too.

Why cat cafés?

The cult-like devotion that cats are given by the Japanese.

The ultra-high stress levels in companies.

Apartments are tiny, making it impossible for most Japanese to have a pet at home.

Kitty Island

On Aoshima Island to the south of Japan, cats outnumber humans six to one. More than 120 felines live on the island alongside about twenty people. Why? In the beginning cats were imported to fight against an invasion of mice in the ancient fishing village. And what happened next? The mice disappeared and the cats multiplied.

A Designer House for Cats

As incredible as it might seem, Asah Kasei, a Japanese firm of architects, had the somewhat extravagant but interesting idea of building a human-sized house (called the Plus-Nyan House), with special features for cats. Thanks to open-air catwalks and climbing steps, cats can keep alert and do their daily gym exercises without even noticing. They even have their own bathrooms!

Happy Cat

Cat's Delight

So that a cat can give its master all the love he or she deserves, it's vital for the cat to be in a comfortable environment. To take care of your cat properly, you have to understand it! Here we will decipher a few key things about our beloved felidae.

The Feline Superpowers

In addition to its one-of-a-kind character, the cat also possesses sensory faculties that fascinate and intrigue us. Learning about them helps to enrich our relationship with our four-footed friend and to understand it better.

1: Nocturnal vision? You mean cats can see in the dark?

Yes, indeed, cats have the capacity to see in the dark (it's called crepuscular vision). You must have noticed that cats' eyes shine in the dark and appear phosphorescent, giving them an almost supernatural appearance. Here's a short explanation.

"A cat at our side is a warm, furry, whiskery, and purring reminder of a lost paradise."

—Lénor Fini

Cats' eyes have three times more light-receptive cells (called cell-rods) than humans'. These cells are responsible for their crepuscular vision in black and white. That's not to say that cats can't see colors, but their color perception is more limited than ours.

Behind the cat's retinas is a reflecting layer of tissue called *tapetum lucidum* (Latin: "bright tapestry"), which increases the quantity of light captured by the retina by 40%.

Therefore, in darkness, a cat's vision is eight times superior to ours. The only fly in the ointment is that cats are less able to focus up close; they can clearly see objects at a starting distance of six inches. They are also more nearsighted than humans.

Finally, a cat's eyes are relatively forward facing, giving it, due to the overlap in the images from each eye, depth perception at the expense of field of view. A cat's peripheral field of vision is slightly superior to ours (around 180° to 160° in humans).

2: Ultra-sensory radar.

We all know that cats have **whiskers** on each side of its upper lip and nose, but did you know that they are called vibrissae and they are also located above the eyes, on the sides of the forehead, on the chin, and on the front legs?

Highly sophisticated sensorial organs, vibrissae are keratin-rich protective skin appendages, like many that are present in humans and animals, such as hair, nails, fur, feathers, and claws. They play a role in positioning the cat's body in space, and they help it as it moves from place to place. Whiskers are able to detect the slightest vibration in the air (whether from humidity, smell, or sound).

3: Impressive hearing.

Hearing is the second most developed sense in cats. A cat hears a very large range of sounds, even slight ones. A cat can hear both low-frequency sounds (infrasound) and high-frequency sounds (ultrasound) from 20,000 hertz to about 60,000 hertz.

This sharp hearing gives it almost "bionic" abilities. Much more sensitive to frequencies than people or dogs are, a cat has the ability to isolate a sound in the middle of other noises and to distinguish the variants in pitch, no matter the sound's intensity.

To do this, it precisely locates the origin and distance by pivoting its ears independent of each other. It can accurately pinpoint a distant sound's location to within an inch or so, or locate a mouse running on the ground 65 feet away.

You can check out this incredible ability when, for example, your cat hears the mailman arrive before you do, or it hears a suspicious noise without you being able to hear anything. If you closely watch its position and its ear movements and learn from them, you might even start to believe that you have supernatural hearing too!

4: A highly developed sense of smell.

Even though it's in third place on the list of sensory powers, after sight and hearing, the cat's **sense of smell** is highly developed. An odor reaches it fast, and the cat will quickly search for the source. If you need convincing of this, try taking a piece of fish out of the fridge and see how fast your cat appears in the kitchen, even if it was far away from the fridge.

A cat's astonishing ability to distinguish smells 50 to 70 times better than we can, even the most complex chemical mixtures, is thanks to two facts. It has more than 200 million olfactory cells (more than a dog, which only has 150 million), and it has specific glands called **Bowman glands.** These activate by secreting a special mucus that humidifies the cat's nose when necessary; for example, when it's hungry. Contrary to popular belief, this dampness has nothing to do with the cat's health or well-being.

Finally, due to the vomeronasal organ or **Jacobson's organ,** a cat has the ability to taste smells. To do this, it wrinkles its muzzle to introduce odors into two small conductors situated behind its incisors, which carry the smell to two fluid-filled sacks in the nasal cavities, which concentrate odors. Smart, eh?

5: A sixth sense?

The question of intuitive communication—or telepathy—between a cat and its master has cropped up for a very long time; some think it's perhaps an ability to emit vibrations that the cat picks up. This idea wasn't born yesterday: even the ancient Egyptians believed that such a method of communication existed.

The following was written on a papyrus discovered in Saqqara:

"When you are thinking, it hears, even if your lips
don't move and even if no words come out of your mouth.
It can read you through the eye of the gods."

In his book *The Unexplained Powers of Animals*,[1] Rupert Sheldrake, a cellular biologist at Cambridge University, demonstrates the existence of an invisible link joining humans, animals, and the environment. The author, who spent five years studying this intuitive communication, asserts that we are all linked together by what he calls a "morphic resonance" that makes telepathic communication possible. According to him, the stronger the affective and emotional links become between two beings, the more the possibility of telepathic exchange increases, the same kind of link that exists between a mother and child.

Numerous moving stories bear witness to this form of communication, and many are recounted in Jean Prieur's book *The Soul of Animals*,[2] such as the astonishing adventure of Amado, a blind cat that travelled 15 miles to find its owner.

Special Herbs for Cats

Although they are carnivores, cats adore certain herbs that have euphoric virtues. Don't get them mixed up with "cat grass," young shoots of grain (wheat or barley) cats use to purge their digestive systems. We're talking about particularly interesting botanical species—plants that make our cats happy.

Valerian *(Valeriana officinalis)* gives off an odor that attracts cats and sets off an immediate and short-lived euphoric frenzy, due to the production of pheromones. To some humans it stinks like old cheese or very smelly socks. You have been warned!

---

1. *Dogs That Know When Their Owners Are Coming Home: And Other Unexplained Powers of Animals* by Rupert Sheldrake (New York: Random House, 2011).
2. *L'Ame des animaux* (The Soul of Animals) by Jean Prieur
   (Paris: Robert Laffont Editions, 2001).

Silver vine *(Actinidia polygama)*, closely related to the kiwi berry, is renowned for eliciting euphoria in cats. It intoxicates 80% of cats and seems to work better on male cats than females.

Catnip *(Nepeta cataria)* is an aromatic plant in the *Lamiaceae* family, which contains a chemical compound called *necpatalactone*, a terpenoid that sets off sex pheromones in the cat's brain.

You can buy these herbs from natural food stores, from herbalists, and in specialty shops. Not all cats react in the same way, so try out a few until you find the plant your cat prefers. You can keep them in an airtight container and give your kitty some once a week as a treat. A festive moment guaranteed!

Cats and Water

A cat's behavior toward water is contradictory, as water both worries them and fascinates them. This could be partly explained by the fact that, having lived a long time in desert regions, cats only got to know bodies of water rather late in their evolution. Even though they are good swimmers, they are not the sort of animal that dives into water to hunt, as the somewhat humorous proverb above suggests. Cats hate being splashed and are more afraid of cold water than warm.

As for drinking water, it is recommended that cats need between 5 and 10 fluid ounces of water per day. Obviously, this amount will vary according to the outside temperature and your feline's activities. Your cat also may get part of that total water intake from its prey, its food, and so on. Cats hate stagnant water so remember to change the water bowl at least every 10 hours.

Finally, you should know that cats like to drink flowing water, including from the tap. It's a fun way for your cat to drink fresh water and an amusing moment for you.

"Cats like fish, but they won't wet their paws."

—10th-century proverb

Being Careful with Food

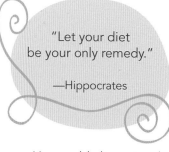

"Let your diet be your only remedy."

—Hippocrates

This axiom is true for humans and also for your cat. If you want your cat to be healthy with beautiful fur, it is essential to take care of its food.

First, you should be particular about the commercial cat food you buy, since its contents often leave a lot to be desired. Don't forget that your cat is a carnivore and that its diet should be varied.

You could alternate a homemade meal (in the evening, for example) with a meal of quality dry food, remembering to leave out a bowl of fresh water at all times. This will help prevent stones in the urinary tract, which can happen frequently in adult cats. When a cat has enough to drink its urine is naturally diluted and stones won't be able to form.

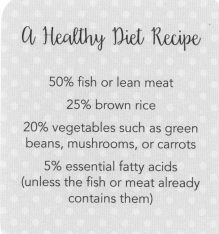

A Healthy Diet Recipe

50% fish or lean meat

25% brown rice

20% vegetables such as green beans, mushrooms, or carrots

5% essential fatty acids (unless the fish or meat already contains them)

There's No Accounting for Taste

Just like humans, each cat has its preferences when it comes to food; some like meat while others prefer fish. So when you adopt a cat, try different types of food until you find those it prefers so that you can prepare meals that blend pleasure and quality.

A Weekly Reward

Every weekend, offer your cat a little present by buying it a food it really likes, such as shrimp (four or five should do depending on its appetite). This festive ritual will make your cat very happy and will create a moment of intense connection between you both. And for an appetizer, you can give it a few small bits of olive—obviously after you've removed the pit.

Forbidden Foods

Dark chocolate: the alkaloid it contains, called theobromine, is poisonous for cats. Less than a third of an ounce could kill a cat, so please be careful!

Vegetables in the Solanaceae family: such as eggplants, peppers, tomatoes, or potatoes. These can cause serious digestive problems.

Vegetables in the Alliacea family: such as leeks, chives, garlic, and shallots. They contain an enzyme that can cause hemorrhages, intestinal pain, and colic.

Avocadoes: they contain persin, a toxic substance that can damage the heart and lungs of our cat friends.

Advice for Silky Fur

First and foremost, beautiful fur is a sign of your cat's good health. And it's a symbol of everything connected to felines.

Remember to supply your cat with the quartet of protein, vitamins, mineral salts, and essential fatty acids necessary to give your cat fur to be proud of.

Nearly a third of the **protein** your cat ingests every day serves to rebuild its skin and its fur. The fur is composed of more than 95% sulfur-containing amino acid–rich proteins. Therefore, a diet that is poor in proteins can lead to a slowing of fur growth, and even to it falling out.

Vitamins A, B5, B6, B10, E, and biotin support fur's vitality. You don't need to give dietary supplements to your cat, but choose a vitamin-rich diet.

Mineral salts, such as copper and zinc, are necessary for the synthesis of keratin, the protein that forms hairs. Give priority to fish, meat, or wheat-based food.

Where to find these vitamins?

Vitamin A: in liver and egg yolk

Vitamin B5: in soy and grains

Vitamin B6: in bran, fish, and wheat germ

Vitamin B10: in green vegetables, grains, and liver

Vitamin E: in grains

Biotin: in yeast and anchovies

Essential fatty acids, such as the omega-6 family, play an important role in maintaining the skin's suppleness and the quality of a cat's fur. The omega-3 family has an anti-inflammatory effect. In addition, certain vitamins such as A and B and certain trace elements such as zinc play a role in different levels in the fur's beauty, and should be in the cat's diet.

A Chef's Trick

Sprinkle powdered brewer's yeast on your cat's food. Rich in vitamin B, amino acids, and trace elements, it will make your cat's fur beautifully silky. You can give your cat half a teaspoon a day for one month.

Brushing, a Moment of Connection

Even if your cat is very clean, it won't hurt it to be brushed at least once a week. This will help it to avoid swallowing too much fur, and will be a nice shared moment between the two of you. Almost all cats love being pampered. To make it easier, begin getting your cat used to being brushed when it is a small kitten.

On the accessories side, use a pin brush for cats, which will help you to gently remove dead hairs. A comb is also a useful tool for smoothing the fur without creating static.

Quiz I Give Up!

1. An ailurophile is someone who...
a) doesn't like cats
b) likes cats
c) is terrified of cats

2. Orange striped cats are...
a) often males
b) often females
c) never females

3. Among the following, which isn't good for cats?
a) green beans
b) dark chocolate
c) rice

4. A tortoiseshell cat is...
a) a male cat with orange/yellow, black, and white fur
b) a male cat with white, black, and orange/yellow fur
c) a female cat with orange/yellow, black, and brown fur

5. A calico is a cat with fur...
a) black and orange/yellow
b) white, black, and orange/yellow
c) white and orange/yellow

6. We call them "tabby cats" when...
a) they are stripey
b) they are wild
c) they are a purebred

7. The record* for proven longevity in a cat is...
a) 26 years old
b) 38 years old
c) 32 years old

8. When a cat is angry its pupils...
a) stay the same
b) dilate
c) retract

9. According to the official book on feline origins in France, there are...
a) 12 different colors in a cat's coat
b) 8 different colors in a cat's coat
c) 9 different colors in a cat's coat

10. Black cats with white paw-pads exist.
a) true
b) false

* According to the *Guinness Book of Records*

11. What do we call a cat whose eyes aren't the same color?
a) a wall-eyed cat
b) an eye-balled cat
c) a bi-colored cat

12. Why do we use the word "crepuscular" in relation to a cat?
a) because it is nearsighted
b) because it has the ability to always land on its feet
c) because it can see in the dark

13. How long is the normal gestation period in a cat?
a) 95 days
b) 46 days
c) 65 days

14. In a litter of five kittens, how many of them could have a different father?
a) none
b) 2
c) 5

15. What is the unique feature of a Manx cat?
a) it doesn't have a tail
b) it has five legs
c) it has red eyes

16. What is the average speed of a cat?
a) 12 miles per hour
b) 50 miles per hour
c) 24 miles per hour

17. What is the name of the cat-headed Egyptian goddess of love and fertility?
a) Hezat
b) Bastet
c) Beset

18. How many claws does a cat have?
a) 10
b) 17
c) 18

19. We speak of allogrooming when several cats...
a) lick each other
b) take a shower together
c) groom in the rain

20. The equivalent age of a human in relation to a 6-year-old cat is...
a) 32 years old
b) 37 years old
c) 40 years old

One of a Kind!

Exploring That Cat Connection

Now that you know all (or almost all) about cats, it's time to explore that unique and multi-faceted connection that links you to your felidae. A shared attitude, a complex language that's just waiting to be deciphered, the mystery of purring's healing power: cats haven't finished amazing us.

The Cat, Finally Recognized as a Sensitive Being

Did you know that not so long ago in the eyes of the law, cats, along with other animals, were considered to be the equivalent of a piece of furniture?

Finally, in 2015, thanks to a petition launched by the 30 Million Friends Foundation and signed by nearly 800,000 people, after two years of intensive debates, the French Parliament awarded the quality of "a living being endowed with sensitivity" to all animals.

This amendment* finally officially recognizes the intrinsic value of animals. Let's hope that this historic turnabout will spread to other nations' legal systems and will put an end to hundreds of years of archaic views concerning animals and their well-being.

Chatting among Friends

Who needs words! Cats have a whole collection of sharp communication tools: tactile, visual, audible, and olfactory.

When addressing other animals, **olfactory communication** comes first, through odors and pheromones the cat secretes, mainly via its paw-pads, the base of its tail, its sides, and the corners of its mouth.

---

* Article 524 modified by Law no. 2015-177, February 16, 2015, article 2.

This olfactory communication is generally accompanied by body positions to underline the message.

On the other hand, in our presence, cats will normally choose **visual, tactile, and audible communication** methods.

Let's examine audible communication first. Did you know that cats emit vocalizations that vary in proportion to its domestication?

The ABCs of Meowing

Contrary to what we might think, a cat doesn't emit just one kind of "meow," but a diversified range, each one having a precise message, but one that's (unfortunately) meaningless to us.

John Bradshaw, a biologist who founded and runs the famous Anthrozoology Institute at Bristol University, has studied the behavior of domestic cats and their owners for more than 25 years. During the course of his studies, he has established a sort of "meow" lexicon; here are a few examples:

When your cat lets out a short crisp meow with its tail in the air, it's to welcome you.
When the meow is drawn out (a sort of "meeeoow") growing softer toward the end, it's a greeting followed by a specific request (food, open the door, I need to go out…).
When your cat states a babbling kind of meow, it's to welcome you and to invite you to join an activity such as a game.

The three main families of vocalizations:

Closed-mouthed vocalizations such as murmuring and purring.

Open-mouthed, becoming progressively closed-mouthed, vocalizations such as mewing.

Open-mouthed vocalizations such as growling, screaming, roaring, hissing, and spitting.

If your cat meows rhythmically and keeps repeating it while backing away rapidly, it means it's protesting over something that's wrong.

Amuse yourself by deciphering the different nuances of meows your cat emits; it will help you to be even more in tune with its needs at any given time. This deciphering isn't simple, but don't forget that meows are always accompanied by physical expressions that are often more explicit, such as the position of its ears or its tail.

On your side, establish the dialogue by replying to your cat either out loud or with a systematic set of signals (like frowning when you aren't pleased). Remember to modulate your voice according to the message you want to get across, and don't forget to be clear, even if it isn't easy to resist the beseeching look in your beloved feline's eyes. It doesn't make much sense calling your cat "sweetie" if you have a firm and maybe disagreeable message to get across to it.

Cats and Conditioned Reflexes

You've probably noticed that your cat comes running, salivating, as soon as it hears the noises associated with you fixing its supper (for example, when you open the refrigerator). Or that it will run and hide as soon as you get out its carrier (or even when you head to the place you keep the carrier), since generally cats don't like travelling or going to the vet.

"A cat puts its heart and soul into purring."

Jean-Louis Hue

Do You Speak Cat?

Deciphering your feline's language isn't easy. Because of this, the Japanese, who certainly aren't lacking in imagination, came up with "Meowlingual," the first cat language translator. According to its marketing explanation, the apparatus is capable of recognizing 200 meows, six moods, and 21 different feline emotions.

And that's not all! It can also be used to check the cat's health, by analyzing 85 different points. On the other hand, there hasn't yet been much feedback about the efficiency of the product.

Count on shelling out about $180 (at the time of its launch) to learn how to speak cat and Japanese—so far the translator isn't adapted for any other language.

While waiting for progress to take another leap forward, you can continue to observe your cat and work to understand it with a simple, low-tech glance...

As Ivan Pavlov demonstrated at the beginning of the 1890s, it's a matter of conditioned reflexes. The physiologist proved that if we accustom a dog to a certain sound to accompany its dinner, it will eventually begin to salivate when it hears the sound, even if no food is served.

You'll notice conditional reflexes in your beloved cat often throughout the day. For example, it quickly understands that it's time to go to bed when you turn off the TV. On a personal note, my three felines dash off toward the stairs the moment I close my laptop. Seeing that it is turned on all day, they quickly understand that when I turn it off it's finally time to go to sleep. I amused myself once by pretending to turn it on again, but Ginger gave me a look that suggested that it was high time I went to bed...

Yes to Purr Therapy!

We have to admit that what we love best about our furbabies is their incredible ability to emit a deep, characteristic vibration that makes us feel good, which we call **purring.** There's no doubt that it has enormously contributed to reinforcing the special link that has joined humans and cats for so long.

What Do We Know about Purring?

It is a very early means of communication, because a kitten, before it's born, picks up on and benefits from the deep purring sounds of its mother.

As soon as a kitten is born, "mommy cat" is careful to emit the well-known, reassuring sound—the famous purr—as often as possible to combat the confusing sounds of the outside world that assault the kitten's ears. On the first day of its life, a kitten is also able to produce its first purrs, which it usually does while feeding.

From the age of three months, a kitten, understanding that purring has a great value, will start using it toward other beings apart from its mother and siblings, to ask for pleasure, food, or comfort.

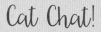

Cat Chat!

Do you think that your cat purrs once in a while? No! Researchers say that a cat actually never stops purring and we only hear it purr when it increases the sound.

A cat is also endowed with sensory receptors called **Pacinian corpuscles,** deeply buried in the hypodermis layer of the skin. Particularly sensitive to vibrations, these receptors rapidly transmit a signal to the brain that produces endorphins, which are beneficial to our four-footed friends.
Our cats are calmed by their own purring!

The Origins of Purring

For a long time scientists thought that purring was due to a vibration of the folds of the larynx. But then they noticed that a cat that had undergone a laryngectomy still purred, so they had to find another explanation.

Nowadays, the most probable theory is that purring is the result of blood movements in the venae cavae, and that's what's responsible for the famous vibrations in the feline's body. Nevertheless, there are still pieces missing from the puzzle, such as the location of the purr center, which still hasn't been identified in the cat's brain.

They Have Their Reasons

Sorry to disappoint you, but cats don't purr with the goal of making us happy. Far from being an altruist, a cat will purr first and foremost for its own well-being.

When we analyze the sound spectrum of a purring cat, we realize that the purring is mainly very deep sounds, at frequencies of 25 to 50 hertz. These are the same frequencies often used for their musical and medical virtues:

Composers also use low frequencies in certain pieces of music to provoke emotions.

Orthopedic doctors have used the action of these frequencies to accelerate the healing of bone fractures and the treatment of osteoarthritis.

Purring's Effect

The use of the term **"purr therapy"** over the last few years leaves us in no doubt about the therapeutic action of purring. Not only does it have a relaxing effect on our four-legged friends, purring also gives us pleasure. We perceive this phenomenon by way of the eardrum and also through the famous Pacinian corpuscles (which we have too). Positive thinking and well-being are transmitted in this way to our brains.[1]

The Virtues of Purring

Contrary to popular belief, **cats don't purr only when they're happy.** Purring also helps calm them in intensely stressful situations.

Researchers at the Animals' Voice Association gathered statistics from veterinary universities showing that in the treatment of wounds and after surgery, cats have five times fewer complications than dogs and they recover three times faster.[2]

Experiencing a cat's purring allows us to evacuate negative energy from our body and works directly on the emotion and memory areas in the brain (hippocampus and amygdala), leading to production of serotonin, the famous hormone of happiness. Serotonin plays a part in sleep quality and our moods and can even help to reduce tiredness caused by jet lag.

Mindfulness Purr Session

If you're lucky enough to have a cat at home you can take advantage of purr sessions several times a day. For optimal benefit, practice a mindfulness session following these directions. It's really very simple: it consists of settling down comfortably in an armchair with your cat on your lap.

Focus your attention on the present moment and think about the sensations you feel when your cat starts purring.

---

1. *Mon chat et moi, on se soigne!* (My cat and I take care of each other!) by Jean-Yves Gauchet (Paris: Le courrier du livre, 2014).
2. Ibid.

Don't forget to breathe deeply to help you achieve this feeling of well-being, and take full advantage of the moment of togetherness. Ten minutes should be enough to start feeling the first benefits. Do as many purr sessions as time allows.

If you don't have a cat handy, no problem—you can use the audio recordings supplied with this book to practice purr therapy. Settle down comfortably in a quiet place and listen to the audio without turning the sound up. Focus your attention on the purring. Relax and take advantage of the healing…

The purring audio is also useful when you're on a bus, on a plane, or anywhere you feel the need to release stress and relax.

Download the audio at http://www.schifferbooks.com/Purrfection.html

Petting

What would your relationship with your cat be like without those wonderful caresses that you give each other? Petting a cat is a shared pleasure, and it's also a great way to reinforce the emotional ties that join human and animal.

"Cats are beings created for storing up caresses."

—Stéphane Mallarmé

It is very difficult to resist plunging your hands into the soft, silky fur of a kitten. (Unless, of course, you don't like cats.) Generally, it knows exactly how to show you when it wants a little attention. It will come and rub against you, give you little head-butts, or confidently stretch out on its back.

On the other hand, don't hesitate to take the initiative yourself; just make sure that you don't disturb it while it's busy with something else—like having a snooze, having a bath, or eating its supper!

Satisfaction

8 Moments of Cat Connection

We domesticate a cat and in turn it tames us. Little by little, we search for each other, we glance at each other, and suddenly, one day, we find each other. As time passes, unbreakable ties are woven, giving way to a relationship full of connection and affection that never stops growing stronger.

In a Glance

My cat and I understand each other in a single glance.

Sometimes, all you need to do is to catch your feline's eye to understand each other. If you are sad, you get the feeling that your cat sympathizes with you; if you're happy, you are certain that it understands and is happy for you.

Tummy Rubs

My cat massages my tummy.

You're lying quietly when suddenly your cat leaps up on the bed, heads straight for your stomach, and, without hesitating, starts "kneading" you with a secret look in its small, sparkling eyes. It's a moment that belongs to just the two of you.

"Happiness is like a cat; if you try to cajole it, it will escape you; if you take no notice of it, it will come and twine itself around your legs and jump onto your lap."

—Robertson Davies

Hand Massage

I slip my fingers between my cat's paw pads.

Have you tried the one-of-a-kind experience of massaging your feline's paw pads? It's a mutually enjoyable moment that allows you to relax and forget daily worries for a while.

Cat on a Perch

My cat jumps onto my shoulders.

It's a pleasant feeling (when your cat isn't too heavy and makes sure to sheath its claws) when you feel the feline dexterity and force in a fraction of a second as your cat leaps onto your shoulders and proudly perches there.

Tech Geek

My cat sleeps behind my computer.

If your feline appreciates the heat put out by a laptop enough to settle down near it for a snooze, you too will be happy. Feeling the positive energy that your cat radiates right next to you is wonderful. From time to time you can sneak a hand around the screen and plunge your fingers into its silky fur. It's a great way of warming your hands up too.

LOL Cat

My cat clowns around to entertain me.

Have you ever noticed that cats have a great penchant for goofing around, especially if they have an audience? They love going into controlled skids on the tile or wood floor, rolling around on the ground, and doing impossible-looking leaps and spectacular somersaults. Your cat is a circus in itself and watching it guarantees you a good time.

Clever Cat

My cat rolls onto its back so that I can give it belly rubs.

Cats like lying on their backs with their paws in the air. Generally, this attitude bears witness to the complete confidence your cat has in you. However, it's also an excellent method of getting you to give it belly rubs. You would be silly not to take advantage of it!

Inspector Cat

My cat reads over my shoulder.

Excessively curious by nature, a cat will never miss the chance to watch your every move. It loves spying on you and annoying you a little at the same time. How about getting your revenge by driving it a little nuts too? How? Tickle it and make faces at it, or tease it gently by wriggling a piece of string in the air just out of its reach.

Between the Two of Us

In Private with My Cat

As French author Colette wrote, "Time spent with a cat is never lost." Contact with cats is a source of intense enrichment. Wake up your animal instincts and give your imagination a loose rein. Learn to understand the cat's tastes, dance and play with it, teach it yoga. There is a vast range of possibilities, and it's up to you to make sure they happen every day.

Signs of Love

Over time you'll establish a unique connection with your kitty that shows itself in various kinds of physical contact that only your cat knows the secret meanings of.

Rubbing Speaks Volumes

When your cat rubs itself against you, it's obviously to show its affection, to get your attention and, more surprisingly, to mark its territory (you) using soothing pheromones. In scientific jargon, we call it familiarization marking or allorubbing.

Affectionate Burrowing

The more your intimacy increases, the more your cat will try to get closer to you, such as by burrowing—a technique that consists of burrowing its head into the hollow of your arm and curling up there for a while.

"My cat is half of my soul."

—Guy Féquant

Eskimo Kisses

When your cat has total confidence in you, it will often show its attachment by a nose-to-nose contact, somewhat like Eskimo kisses. It's generally on the cool side but pretty nice—even when you've just woken up!

Kneading

It's kind of a funny word to use in association with a cat, but the action explains it. It's a form of kneading that your cat will carry out, with its claws slightly unsheathed, on a carefully selected surface—often a blanket, a rug, a piece of clothing, and also you, as a sign of affection. This is a regressive pleasure: a kitten has a habit of kneading its mother's teats during the first months of its life.

Feline Stretching

The least we can say is that in the area of well-being, cats have nothing to learn from us. They know perfectly well what is good for them and they know how to put it into practice every day: numerous naps—a cat sleeps around 16 hours a day; playing, to look on the bright side of life; daily gymnastic exercises through regular stretching sessions to keep their joints springy and to reactivate their energy after a satisfying snooze.

Cat Stretching

Why not copy your cat by practicing cat positions? As your cat already knows, it's an ideal way to stretch your back and neck, to work on pelvic suppleness, to increase the fluidity of energy in your backbone, and to go with the flow.

Find somewhere quiet where you won't be interrupted, and wear something loose and comfortable. Practice the following sequence: Get on your hands and knees, knees slightly lower than your hips, and your hands slightly higher than your shoulders. Your back should be straight, your neck relaxed, and your face toward the floor.

1

Take a deep breath and slowly lift your head, hollowing your back as much as possible. Be careful: you shouldn't feel any pain. Hold your breath for two seconds.

2

Breathe out slowly, rounding your back and slowly lowering your head towards the floor. Hold your breath for two seconds.

3

Each repetition should last three or four seconds. Repeat the exercise five or six times. With each new breath, try to hollow out and round your back a little more. Visualize your cat to check that your positioning is correct.

My Cat, the Yogi Master

Do you like yoga, and do you practice it on your own at home? What if you shared this beneficial activity with your beloved feline, who could quickly become the ideal partner?

Not only will practicing yoga together reinforce the connection between you and kitty, but it will stop your cat from trying to distract you—a favorite pastime when it feels left out.

As you probably know, yoga invites you, through poses, to control your breathing and to do concentration and visualization exercises. The aim is to improve your physical and emotional balance while optimizing harmony among the body, the mind, and the spirit.

The objective isn't to make things uncomfortable, so alternate your poses between ones where you hold your cat and freer poses where your cat could climb onto your back, for example.

For poses where you can't carry your cat, trust it and let it react as it wants. Both player and acrobat, it will probably quickly surprise you by its astonishing choreographies. You can find great (and touching) videos on the Internet of yoga sessions between owner and cat.

Yoga Poses Where You Can Hold Your Cat

Prayer pose
(*Pranamasana*)

Raised arms pose
(*Hasta Uttanasana*)

Chair pose (*Utkatasana*)

Warrior pose (*Virabhadrasana*)

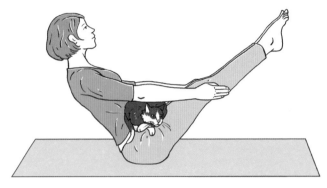

Boat pose (*Navasana*)

Tree pose (*Vrksasana*)

You could finish your yoga session with the Savasana pose. Lie flat on your back with legs slightly apart, toes pointing outward, arms parallel to your body but not touching it, palms upward. Close your eyes and breathe slowly and deeply. With a little training, your feline won't take long to settle on your stomach for a closing cuddle.

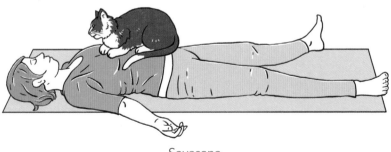

Savasana

Fun Activities to Share

Even though your cat is a big sleeper, it is also a big playmate whose imagination and creativity are without limits. Although your cat is resourceful enough to play alone, it really loves playing with you, so don't miss the fun. It's an excellent way of giving yourself a breather during a busy day.

Sometimes it may be your cat who comes to find *you* so that you can play together. Cats have a way of being able to gauge our equilibrium, and will find a gentle way of saying, "Come and play (or come to bed), you've done enough for today!"

Generally the toys bought in stores are expensive, and our four-legged friends, always looking for new things, quickly get bored with them. So use homemade toys that you can easily make from various recycled objects (odd socks, old shoe-laces, small fluffy things, old bathrobe belts, toilet roll tubes that you can join together to make a slithering snake…) or objects found outside (small pieces of wood, dead branches, pine cones…).

Because making toys for cats is child's play, don't hesitate to get your kids to help you make them. Not only is it fun, it's a good excuse to make a mess!

Think About It

Do you think that your cat doesn't like to play? You're mistaken. All cats love playing, but some are lazier than others. Get your cat used to playing little by little and you'll see that it will quickly develop its innate taste for fun.

Games Kitty Loves

Playing hide-and-seek in tight places, especially in cardboard boxes.

Getting into wrapping paper.

Unrolling the toilet paper.

Playing with ribbons or bits of string.

Sled riding: the cat sits on a bag or a jacket (pretty much anything will work) and you pull it along.

Playing soccer with table tennis balls.

Pretending to be a fishing rod.

.....

Careful! Don't leave swallowable small toys lying around.

Homemade Toys

Toilet paper cylinders.

Paper balls made from old newspapers.

Corks (once they've been cleaned so that no wine is left on them).

The plastic rings that are part of juice bottle and water bottle tops.

The bottle tops themselves.

Any other object that will roll and amuse your kitty.

Long Live Boxes!

If you're lucky enough to have a cat, you've obviously noticed that it loves getting into any cardboard box it comes across, even if they are not quite its size. But have you ever asked yourself where this passion comes from? Well, researchers at Utrecht University[*] tackled the question with a study. They separated twenty cats into two groups. One group had boxes, the other group didn't.

After observing the cats' behavior, they discovered that the cats that had boxes were less stressed and more sociable than the others. This is likely due to the fact that in the wild, a cat can find lots of places to hide from enemies and deal with stress, places that their domesticated counterparts don't have. Boxes are perfect substitutes.

* Source: www.wamiz.com

The Gourmet Game That Will Drive Your Cat Wild

Get a small plastic bottle (like a small water bottle), dry it out, and fill it with dry food. It's ready! Your cat will bat it and roll it all over trying to get at its precious contents.

Toys Most Cats Don't Like

Noisy toys: the ones that squeak or make mechanical noises.

Toys that look like birds, mice, or fish.
(That's right, our beloved felidae don't like looking like fools!)

Toys that are a little worn out, because cats like new things and have a taste for luxury products!

Toys that you buy for yourself and not for your cat!
Remember that it's not always the best-looking toys that make your cat happy.

Workshop!

DIY Toy Kitty Fishing Rod

You don't need to rush to the store to amuse your cat! Here is a 100% natural fishing rod that will create great down time with your kitty.

Materials

1 wooden stick about 12 in. long
1 piece of string about 3 ft. long
1 pom-pom

Instructions

1. Tie the pom-pom to one end of the string.
2. Tie the other end firmly to the end of the stick.
3. It's ready. Now you can go fishing!

Cat Online 2.0

With millions of cats and millions of homes equipped with a computer, it would be difficult for cats to ignore cyber mania. They're not only crazy about computers—with a mischievous pleasure in monopolizing them—but our beloved kitties have become stars of a large number of apps and interactive games dedicated to them. Not to mention selfies, which they can now take on their own thanks to the ingenuity of smartphone creators. Zoom in on a cyber-phenomenon.

Cyberattraction

Admit it, over the years computers have become a real extension of ourselves. We spend a lot of time in front of the screen, and cats seem to have become addicted too, but not for the same reasons.

In general, cats are fairly possessive, and they like having a lot of attention paid to them. The fact that we spend so much time in front of the screen obviously makes them a little (or a lot) jealous. Coming to annoy us is the best way they've found of getting our attention.

Several No-fail Techniques

Rubbing itself against the computer screen (especially if it's a laptop) to distract you and at the same time leave a few hairs and pheromones behind.

Lying across the keyboard.

Tapping on (or even kneading) the keys so that we can't write anything legible. It's as though cats like the massage they get from keyboard keys.

Cats like the heat put out by computers, just as they like any other heat source. A great way to stop your cat from pestering you (too much), but keeping him at your side, is to put a small blanket or a folded bath towel behind your laptop. Not only will you be able to work without fear of being interrupted, but you'll also quickly find that the presence of your cat greatly improves your sense of well-being.

Kitty Apps

These days, communicating with one's cat can be done via a virtual world where the feline weaves its web. This is done through numerous more-or-less successful apps. Here are the best of them—the crème de la crème, I might say.

A True Story

I spend long hours in front of my computer and one of my three cats, Ginger, spends a large part of the day asleep behind it. Sometimes I feel my energy draining away and often I've noticed that this happens when Ginger isn't there.

You'll also notice that a cat, naturally mischievous, is attracted to your mouse's cursor. If you want your cat to leave you in peace, download an app that it can consult on your tablet. There's no stopping progress!

A Selfie for Cats

Are you hooked on selfies? If the answer is yes, don't be surprised to learn that your cat might want to take part in this activity too. To flatter it, but also for your own pleasure, there's a free app that will allow your feline to take its own photo with a simple click. The idea is simple: a small red light moves across the screen on your smartphone to attract your cat, which plants its paw on the screen and takes the photo. Without knowing it, your cat has just taken its first selfie.

Cat Snaps—free app available for iOS and Android.

My Cat Selfie

Would you like to give a slightly feline touch to your selfies? Then the Catwang app was made for you. Thanks to this app you can add some "cat-itude" to your selfies and other photos. Not for the fainthearted, because the visuals are taken from the collection of the alternative hip hop collective Old Future created by the California rapper Tyler, The Creator.

Catwang—free app available for iOS and Android.

Hunting 2.0

Cats love playing but don't always have the opportunity to get outside and chase mice. It's because of this that a famous brand of cat food has created several games for cats that can be downloaded onto your tablet. Thus your cat can hunt fish, birds, and insects virtually. So that you won't feel left out, the app also allows you to challenge your kitty with an option called "You vs. Cat." The only fly in the ointment is the risk of scratch marks on your iPad screen.

Games for Cats—free app available for iOS.

Speak Cat

After the translator mentioned earlier to better understand your felidae, here is the translator for it to understand you! Your cat will never be able to turn a deaf ear again.

This app allows you to instantly translate the master's words into meows, thanks to 175 recordings of 25 different cats. The translation app also includes a harmony table which will allow you to instantly access 16 of the best-known cat sounds. This translator promises hilarious times!

Human-to-Cat Translator—free app available for iOS and Android.

Google Maps for Cats

Created by an art teacher at a university in Florida, this site offers a procedure similar to Google Maps, but with photos of cats posted by Instagram members. You can spend hours perusing an interactive map that shows pictures of cats from every country with or without their owners. A great way to geolocate all the cats in the world—or almost…

www.iknowwhereyourcatlives.com

Cats and IRL (In Real Life) Encounters

Having a cat is an excellent means of enjoying yourself and encouraging interesting encounters. How? By joining a pet (and owner) dating site or by throwing a kitten shower.

Dating Sites for Cats

Did you know that there are dating sites for cats? Surfing the trend, these sites play the role of arranging meetings for owners rather than their pets.

For example, the PetsDating site allows you to organize walks with other pet owners and to join a real community, as well as offering a number of services: a social networking system (a sort of Facebook for animals), meetings between members via the organization of walks, and more.

Examples: www.petsdating.com and fr.yummypets.com

A Kitten Shower

You've just adopted a kitten, or soon will be? To mark this momentous occasion, organize a kitty shower along the model of a baby shower.

A kitten shower is an excellent event for showing off your kitten to your friends, and for receiving little gifts that will amuse it every day. Along with all the fun, you'll be able to find out if there's a willing cat lover among your friends who will be willing to look after your kitty during your vacations. It's a good idea to work this detail out as soon as possible!

Online Catnip

Does it break your heart leaving your cat alone at home? Would you like to keep in touch with it even when you're at work? Do you dream of being a fly on the wall so that you can see what your cat gets up to while you're not there? Take a look at these great resources!

Tracking Your Cat

If you're lucky enough to have a yard, your cat probably likes to explore the neighborhood from time to time. Did you know that you can buy cameras for cats that allow you to track them and find out all the secrets of their daily and nocturnal adventures? Thanks to GPS technology, smart devices can locate your cat while it's outside. The data is transmitted in real time and lets you finally understand your cat's daily activities.

Our choice: www.eyenimal.com

Never without My Cat

Did you know that apps exist that allow you to interact with your feline long-distance? For example, the smart device Kittyo has a camera, speakers, a laser pointer, and a compartment full of treats. You can connect it to your smartphone after downloading the app, which is available on iOS or Android.

With it you can film your cat, talk to it, set off noises to attract its attention, feed it—all from your smartphone. You can remotely move the laser pointer around and your cat can spend happy times trying to catch it.

For more information: www.kittyo.com

Sport at a Distance

This looks like a small cube with an integrated wide-angle camera, microphone, and speakers. This smart device also has a laser pointer so you can play with your cat at a distance and get it to do its exercises when you're not at home. Great, huh?

For more information: www.petcube.com

Chatting with Your Cat

Yes, you can chat with your cat via a videophone. All you have to do is plug it in and attach it to the wall. Then you connect by Wi-Fi via an app you download onto your smart phone (iOS or Android), a computer, or a tablet. When you want to talk to your kitty, just go onto the app and start a video call. An ultrasonic alarm goes off and attracts your cat to the videophone.

For more information: www.petchatz.com

A Connected Litterbox to Check Your Cat's Health

Imagine a high-tech base that looks a lot like a kitchen scale and that you place under your ordinary litterbox. All you need to do is to synchronize the scales with an app. Then you'll know your cat's weight, its production rate of organic waste, the number of visits to the litterbox, and the box's cleanliness level, all in real time.

The data gives a visual analysis of your cat's health profile, mainly through its weight curve. It's a simple and efficient way to detect early health problems without disturbing your four-legged friend.

For more information: www.tailio.com

Feline Accessories

Not so long ago, posing with one's cat or wearing a fashion accessory with a feline on it wasn't really the fashionable thing to do and was the sort of thing only an old aunt or a cat lady would dare to wear! But that was before…

Today, animals, and especially cats, are uncontested fashion stars and can be found decorating their humans in all shapes and forms: cat-shaped rings, cat-adorned socks, t-shirts, tote bags, dresses, underwear, and much more…

Cats belonging to celebrities also become VIPs, like Choupette, the beautiful blue-eyed white cat belonging to the famous fashion designer Karl Lagerfeld. A book has even been written about Choupette.

More than ever, cats make fashion purr. Show your creative claws and get into craft mode by trying these four very fashionable creations!

You'll find the patterns on pages 82–85. All you need to do is photocopy them, enlarging them to the size you want.

Project difficulty levels:

★ easy
★★ medium
★★★ hard

Workshop!
Meow 2.0 T-shirt

Difficulty level: ★ ★

Time: about 2 hours

Cost: about $20 to $25 depending on the T-shirt

Techniques used: customizing and sewing

Customized T-shirts are especially stylish and look great with jeans, a jacket, and pretty shoes. Our design is very graphic and should make everyone want to copy you!

Materials

- 1 solid-color T-shirt
- 1 iron-on denim patch, dark blue
- 1 iron-on denim patch, light blue
- 1 small piece of pale pink fabric
- Magenta wool (for felting)
- Felting needle
- Yellow embroidery floss
- Scissors
- Iron
- Fabric pencil
- Fabric glue

Instructions

1. Using a photocopy of the pattern, cut out shape 1 and position it on the dark blue iron-on denim. Trace around the pattern. Cut the piece out.

2. Using a photocopy of the pattern, cut out shape 2 and position it on the light blue iron-on denim. Trace around the pattern. Cut the piece out.

3. Place the two shapes (1 & 2) on the T-shirt, as shown in the photo.

4. Position the two shapes and iron them onto your T-shirt with a hot iron until they adhere to the cloth.

The Insides of the Ears

1. Using a photocopy of the pattern, cut out shape 3 and position it on the pale pink fabric. Trace around the pattern. Repeat. Cut the 2 pieces out.

2. Using the needle, apply the wool, needle felting it onto the ears.

3. Glue the felted ears in place using fabric glue.

All you need to do now is to embroider the nose and mouth of your cat with the yellow floss.

Workshop!
Copper Kitty T-shirt

Difficulty level: ★

Time: about 1 hour

Cost: about $20 to $25 depending on the T-shirt

Techniques used: textile painting and stenciling

Long-sleeved T-shirts are no longer reserved for relaxing on Sundays. They look great with anything you might wear during the week, and can be oversized or figure-hugging. Here's a copper version of a rather cross kitty.

Materials

- 1 solid-color T-shirt
- Copper-colored fabric paint
- Black fabric pen
- 1 sheet of card stock
- Pencil
- Utility knife

Instructions

1. Copy the pattern onto the card stock.

2. Cut the shape out with the utility knife.

3. Position the stencil on your T-shirt and paint the inside area with the copper paint.

4. Draw in the whiskers, and add a few hairs with the black textile pen.

Workshop!
Felidae Totebag

Difficulty level: ★
Time: about 2 hours
Cost: less than $15
Techniques used:
textile painting

Totebags are practical, ecological, and (in this case) stylish. This very feline version is sure to make your friends green with envy.

Materials

- Black textile ink
- 1 iron-on denim patch, black
- Organic-cotton tote bag
- 1 sheet of card stock
- Pencil

Instructions

The design on the front side

1. Make your stencils in the same way as in the preceding project.

2. Place the half-cat shape (1) stencil onto the tote bag and paint the inside area.

3. Place the decorative shape (2) near the stencilled cat and paint the inside area. Repeat, arranging them to form a decorative pattern.

The pocket on the back side

1. Using a photocopy of the pattern, cut out the pocket shape and position it on the black iron-on denim. Trace around the pattern. Cut the piece out.

2. Fold back a half-inch border around the pocket. Iron to adhere only the edges.

3. To finish, sew the bottom edges of the pocket onto the back side of the bag.

Workshop!

Never without My Cat Notebook

Difficulty level: ★

Time: about 1 hour

Cost: less than $10

Techniques used: Collaging

It's a good idea to take notes, but it's better when you write them in an ultra-fashionable customized notebook! This graphic cat notebook should help to inspire you.

Materials

- 1 7" × 10" notebook
- 1 paper cat stencil (see patterns)
- Utility knife
- Repositionable glue
- Patterned paper
- Glitter paper
- 1 sheet of card stock
- Pencil

Instructions

1. Make your cat stencil by tracing the pattern onto heavy paper and cutting it out.

2. With the repositionable glue, stick the stencil on the back of one of your sheets of decorative paper. Using the utility knife, cut out the head and the bowtie and other open shapes.

3. Repeat this six times with different papers, to get 6 cat's heads in various patterns.

4. Cut out a rectangle of 6" × 10" from the card stock (for a 7" × 10" notebook). Fold the rectangle in half and glue it onto the notebook's spine.

5. To finish, position and glue down your cat heads, one above the other. Stick three on the front and three on the back of the notebook.

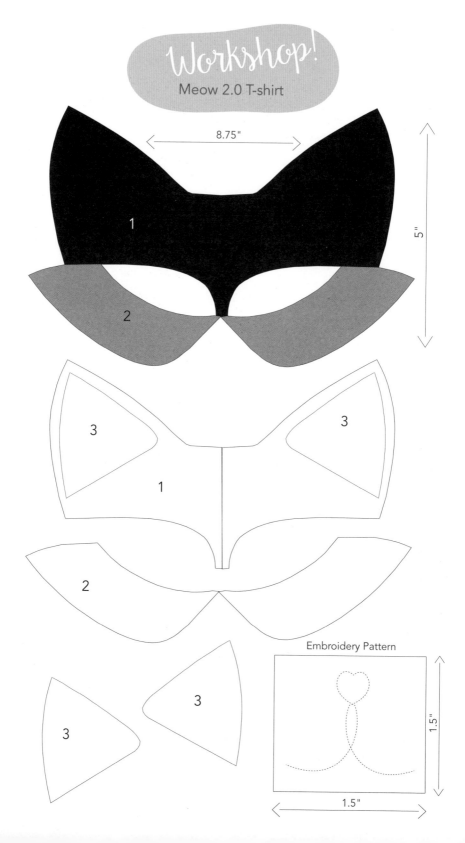

Workshop!

Meow 2.0 T-shirt

8.75"

1

5"

2

3   3

1

2

3   3

3

Embroidery Pattern

1.5"

1.5"

6.75"

8.25"

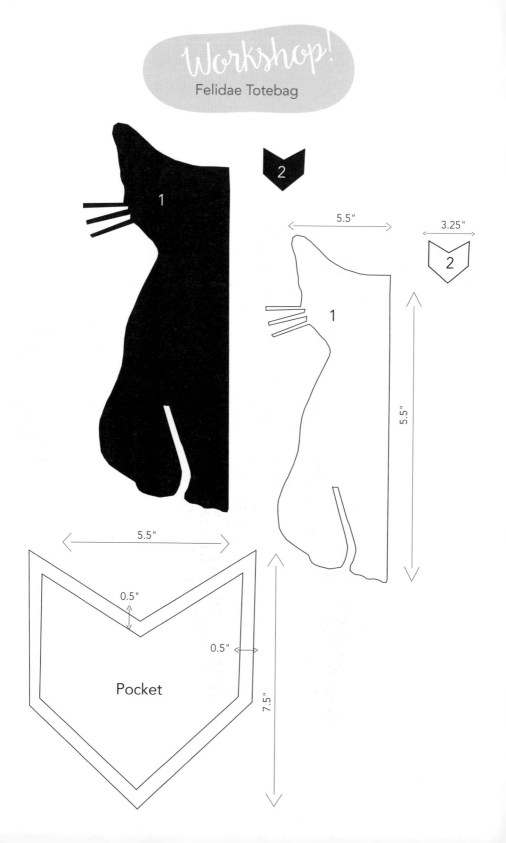

Workshop!

Felidae Totebag

2

1

5.5"

3.25"

2

1

5.5"

5.5"

0.5"

0.5"

Pocket

7.5"

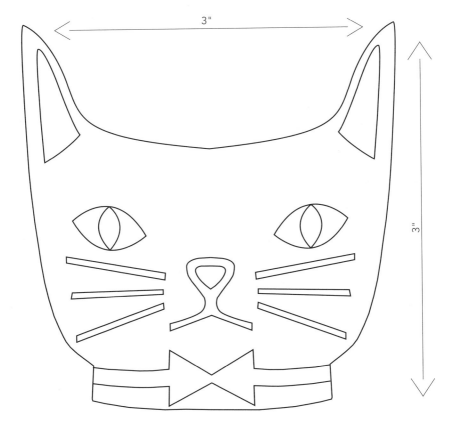

3"

3"

The author and the editor
would like to thank CreaVea and Toga
for the supplies that allowed us to
make these items.

CreaVea—www.creavea.com

The products used were:
Iron-on light blue denim patch A4—ref. 00052466 (T-shirt)
Iron-on dark blue denim patch A4—ref. 00052467 (T-shirt)
Iron-on black denim patch A4—ref. 00052464 (T-shirt)
Magenta wool 100g—ref. 01305452 (T-shirt)
Cotton floss, Fun assortment, 12 skeins of 8m—ref. 00056281 (T-shirt)
Mahé fabric glue 30ml—ref. 00031939 (T-shirt)
Pébéo Setacolor fabric paint 45ml copper color—ref. 00056281 (copper T-shirt)
Setasckrib+ black fine-point textile pen for light colored cloth—ref. 00029298 (copper T-shirt)
Ki-Sign black fabric ink with applicator 30ml—ref. 00011801 (copper T-shirt)

Toga—www.toga-shop.com

The products used were:
Notebook to decorate, kraft cover, 80 pages, 17x24cm—ref. Su48 (notebook)
Permanent repositionable glue pen, large tip—ref. GZ03 (notebook)
Permanent repositionable glue pen, medium tip—ref. GZ02 (notebook)
Permanent repositionable glue pen, fine tip—ref. GZ01 (notebook)
Various sheets of Mahé paper (notebook)
Glitter paper anthracite 1 sheet—ref. PE102 (notebook)
Glitter paper copper 1 sheet—ref. PE93 (notebook)

Thanks also to Marie Bouquin
for her talent and creativity.

Useful Info

To round off this book, I invite you to discover a few feline curiosities and addresses, ones that will make cat lovers happy. It's an excellent way of continuing this very special relationship that connects us to our cats.

Feline Places

A Cat Bar in Paris

Following the success of Neko Cafés shops in Japan, it wasn't long before the concept spread to other places.

The Café des Chats was one early example. Two locations opened in Paris in 2013.

The café is a tea shop and restaurant in which a dozen cats, all adopted from shelters, live freely 24/7, without any restrictions as to their movements within the café (aside, of course, from the kitchen). They were all chosen for their sociable natures toward other cats and humans. The cats are all spayed or neutered, vaccinated, and have health insurance. A part of the profits the café makes is donated to feline protection organizations, and every month a contribution is made to a retirement account for each cat.

In the selection process, the priority isn't necessarily the cat's color or softness of its fur, nor its gorgeous eyes. No, the only criterion is the future well-being of these felines in the café.

So that the cats are left in peace, cat cafés have certain very strictly followed rules. The Paris cafés' rules reflect the standard rules you'll find in cat cafés around the world.

The cats mustn't be disturbed or handled while they are sleeping. The cats have a number of shelves quite high up, out of human reach, to satisfy their need for independence and calm.

It's prohibited to pick up or carry the cats. On the other hand, they have the right to jump onto your lap, purr there, or get down and meow. Here, the cats rule.

No feeding the cats, because the consequences could be disastrous for their health. High-quality cat food and fresh water from the fountain are available for them.

Hygiene measures are also very strict. An alcohol-based hand sanitizing gel is available for clients at the front door. The management of the Animal Protection League has approved the café in terms of the cats' well-being. The cats have a room with litterboxes, completely separate from the café, and accessible via a cat flap. The boxes are cleaned out several times a day.

Margaux Gandelon, the brains behind the Parisian concept, took two mandatory training courses to be able to open the café: CETAC (a certificate for technical studies in pets) and the restaurant food hygiene certification.

Finally, for obvious reasons, dogs and other cats aren't allowed in the café.

My Visit to the Café des Chats, Paris

It was a miserable afternoon; it was raining cats and dogs, so I decided to try out the new café in rue Sedaine in the Bastille district of Paris. On my arrival I noticed a Maneki Neko, the good luck figurine and a nod to the famous Neko Cafés in Japan, on a counter by the door. In the large room in front of me, there were already a dozen adults and a few children, all excited to see the 15 cats there.

I chose to sit at a coffee table thinking that the cats would be more likely to come and keep me company there. There was a really warm atmosphere in the café. The clients were all smiling and they kept getting up to go and pet a cat or two. Once settled, I was happy to watch other people coming into the café: somewhat intimidated at first, their attitude changed quickly and they seemed to relax in the feeling of well-being radiating from the cats.

In turn, I began to relax and feel all my stress melt away; I let myself be calmed by the protective aura surrounding the cats in the room, when suddenly Artemis and Apollo jumped onto the sofa where I was sitting and looked at me tenderly. These two seemed to be very close and I soon found out that they were brother and sister. The waiter told me a very moving story: Apollo had been abandoned in front of the café's window, where he found Artemis, who was already a lodger in the café. So I understood why they were so inseparable. For a few minutes we cuddled and gazed intently into each other's eyes. I relaxed completely and didn't even notice time passing. I just felt good, and I could have stayed there for hours. I took a few photos (like all the other clients), and sadly, it was already time to leave.

As soon as I stepped out the café's door, still glowing from my experience, I was planning my next visit.

Call of Nature:
Ecological, Fun, and Biodegradable Litterboxes

Is the litterbox doomed to become a thing of the past? It's a good question to ask when you notice the new concepts that flourish on the feline market. We fell in love with an innovative product: disposable, biodegradable litterboxes.

It comes ready to use, and takes just a couple of seconds to set up—child's play really, and ideal for busy pet owners who are in a rush but still have an ecological spirit.

Most cats don't need to be encouraged, and adopt this new litterbox's concept immediately. An all-in-one idea, delivered with a little shovel and litter, it's sturdy enough to withstand being assaulted by the most ferocious feline, and you can change the litter without getting your hands dirty.

The litter has been specially formulated and is ultra-absorbent thanks to the wood fibers in it. The damp litter dissolves into very fine sawdust which falls to the bottom of the box. After a week of use, you simply fold the box and put it out in the trash. It biodegrades.

For more information: www.poopycat.com and www.facebook.com/poopycat/

Toilet Seat for Cats

Do you ever wish that your cat would just "go to the bathroom" like you? Your wish can come true thanks to a complete kit to help you train your feline to use the toilet for its needs. Award-winning, it's been developed with help from vets, animal behavior specialists, and cat breeders.

It's a three-stage process to train cats to use human toilets and get rid of the litterbox in your home.

The kit comes with three training discs (red, orange, and green), an instruction booklet, and a 30-minute video with step-by-step training instructions.

At the end of the training period, the cat should be able to use the bathroom without any added training disc. You just have to remember not to leave the bathroom door shut. I wonder when they'll invent a training method for flushing afterwards.

For more information: www.litterkwitter.com

Cat Health Insurance

Animal health insurance is the equivalent of human health insurance. It isn't required, but it helps owners face vet bills when cats need care. Treatment for animals is expensive, and the bill can rise rapidly. Certain owners are sometimes unable to take their pet to the vet, because they just don't have the funds.

For cats, health insurance should be taken out before the cat reaches five years of age (sometimes the age limit is eight years if the cat lives in an apartment).

Depending on the plan chosen, reimbursement rates can range from 50% to 100%. Insurance premium prices vary and sometimes increase as your cat ages. The differences in prices sometimes hide large differences in the coverage for your cat, so shop carefully.

It's a good idea to carefully read the details and compare prices before taking out a health insurance policy.

Several insurance companies for animals have opened, but some standard insurance companies are also beginning to offer cat coverage policies. Ask your veterinarian or other pet owners for some insurance companies to consider, or look online.

Index

Acknowledgments

With thanks to...

Juliette Magro and Dominique Poussielgue for having confidence in me; my parents for their unfailing support; Georges for his patience and precious help; Marie Bouquin for her creative talent; and all cat lovers who inspired me while writing this book.

. . . .

Through her professional experience, Sophie Macheteau, consultant and author of several books, has developed expertise in the area of well-being. A cat lover since childhood and owner of three adorable felidae, it's only natural that she decided to write this book.